Talking to Myself
. . . writing down the inner voice
A Woman's Journal

HAZELDEN®

ACKNOWLEDGMENTS:
Hazelden would like to express appreciation and
give special thanks to Jan Borene and Frank Giamarese
for their help in creating this journal.
Our thanks also to Morgan Brooke for her
book design and illustrations.

Hazelden Educational Materials
Center City, Minnesota 55012-0176

ISBN: 0-89486-862-4

Editor's note
Hazelden Educational Materials offers
a variety of information on chemical dependency
and related areas. Our publications do not necessarily
represent Hazelden's programs, nor do they officially
speak for any Twelve Step organization.

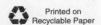 Printed on
Recyclable Paper

P ierre said, "We imagine that when we are thrown out of our usual ruts, all is lost, but it is only then that what is new and good begins. While there is life, there is happiness."

WAR AND PEACE, LEO TOLSTOY

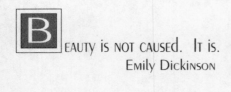

BEAUTY IS NOT CAUSED. IT IS.
Emily Dickinson

I have adopted as my motto the disclaimer often found on clothes made of COTTON OR RAW silk. "This GARMENT is made from 100 PERCENT NATURAL fibers. Any iRREGULARity OR VARIATION is NOT TO be considered defective. Imperfections ENHANCE THE beauty of THE fabric."

WOMEN'S BOOK OF COURAGE

Experiencing the present with the whole of my body instead of with the pinpoint of my intellect led to all sorts of new knowledge and new contentment.

A Life of One's Own, Joanna Field

The child who tries to create a choice that is outside the family's repertoire can expect to be exhausted for at least two years.

Blue Rise, Rebecca Hill

We trust memory against all evidence; it is selective, subjective, cannily defensive, unreliable as fact.

A Romantic Education, Patricia Hampl

T HESE MEN, IT'S NOT LIKE WE DON'T SEE THEM COMING.
OUR INTUITION IS GOOD; THE PROBLEM IS WE IGNORE IT.
REASON TO LIVE, AMY HEMPEL

Weaving a cocoon out of the substance of one's own life is the necessary prerequisite for the emergence of psyche: in withdrawing we prepare a way out.

The Moon and the Virgin, Nor Hall

T he eagle and the serpent are at war in me
The serpent fighting for blind desire
The eagle for clarity

Don Juan's Reckless Daughter, Joni Mitchell

The ultimate goal of life remains the spiritual growth of the individual, the solitary journey to peaks that can be climbed only alone.

The Road Less Traveled, M. Scott Peck

I came to explore the wreck.
The words are purposes.
The words are maps.
I came to see the damage that was done
and the treasures that prevail.
Diving into the Wreck, Adrienne Rich

WHEN I'M SCARED AND UNCERTAIN,
I'M MOST VULNERABLE TO BELIEVING
THAT SOMEONE SOMEWHERE MUST BE
SMART ENOUGH TO KNOW WHAT'S BEST FOR ME
AND STRONG ENOUGH TO TAKE CARE OF ME.
AN END TO INNOCENCE, SHELDON KOPP

I began to understand that self-esteem isn't everything; it's just that there's nothing without it.

Revolution From Within, Gloria Steinem

Failures loom large and ominous,
and sucesses look like specks on the horizon,
mere accidents of nature.

Women's Book of Courage

The culture dishes up an all-or-nothing proposition, disguised as the chance to have it all: a female must forfeit family attachments for a career or forgo achievements that lie beyond the walls of the household.

The Girl Within, Emily Hancock

Exposing who we really are invites judgment, sometimes rejection, oftentimes discounting.

Each Day a New Beginning

I HAVE NEVER MET A WOMAN WHO FELT SHE
WAS beautiful . . . and I know beautiful WOMEN.
A ROMANTIC EDUCATION, PATRICIA HAMPL

Being a good friend to ourselves means that we have
the courage to stop crippling ourselves with criticism
and learn, instead, to compliment and congratulate ourselves.

Women's Book of Courage

What woman needs is not as a woman to act or rule, but as a nature to grow, as an intellect to discern, as a soul to live freely and unimpeded, to unfold such powers as were given to her when we left our common home.

Margaret Fuller

I now mother my mother when I can no longer mother my daughter who is older than I have ever felt myself to be.

Susan Jacobson

It has taken me all the time I've had to become myself, yet now that I'm old, there are times when I feel I am barely here, no room for me at all. I remember that in the last months of my pregnancies the child seemed to claim almost all my body, my strength, my breath, and I held on wondering if my burden was my enemy, uncertain whether my own life was at all mine. Is life a pregnancy? That would make death a birth.

The Measure of My Days, Florida Scott-Maxwell

We clothe events with the drapery of our thoughts.

As a Man Thinketh, James Allen

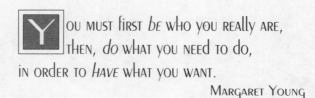

You must first *be* who you really are,
then, *do* what you need to do,
in order to *have* what you want.

Margaret Young

I want to speak out of my heart. I am so afraid not to be heard, so afraid to be heard.

TERESA C.

ot the destination, but the willingness to wander in pursuit characterizes pilgrimage.

Spillville, Patricia Hampl

A popular misconception is that we can't change the past—everyone is constantly changing their own past, recalling it, revising it.

The Diviners, Margaret Laurence

At the same time I'm thinking that I have to let go.
What you have to decide, really, is whether to be crazy or not,
and I haven't the stamina, the pure, seething will, for prolonged craziness.

Moons of Jupiter, Alice Munro

Obsession is solitary madness, self-imposed suffering, a prison camp built for one. Why do we do this? Damned if I know. Someone obviously dropped us on our collective heads when we were babies.
Sex Tips for Girls, Cynthia Heimel

You won't find your inner truth while analyzing, talking, or trying to figure out other people.
Women, Sex, and Addiction, Charlotte Davis Kasl

I think the idea of inner authority is upsetting
to those accustomed to looking outside for orders,
and certainly to those accustomed to giving them.
Revolution From Within, Gloria Steinem

Other people can be very complimentary and supportive, but if we secretly know we're worthless, their words slide off as if we were teflon-coated.

WOMEN'S BOOK OF COURAGE

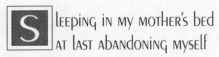leeping in my mother's bed
at last abandoning myself
to the peace
and the breast
of the one who knows me as herself—
and I am safe.

Yesterday I Saw The Sun, Ally Sheedy

I think I am ready to begin returning from the depths. I have plummeted about as far as I wish to for this week, this month, this lifetime.

Teresa C.

Like honesty, compassion may be expressed through verbal means but its basic form of communication is silence.

Loneliness and Love, Clark E. Moustakas

I learned to know something about my anger, my shyness, my loneliness, my sense of ineptness. And I learned not to feel defeated when acknowledging any one or all of them.

Always a Woman, Kaylan Pickford

Passionate investment leaves us vulnerable to loss.
And sometimes, no matter how clever we are, we must lose.

Necessary Losses, Judith Viorst

I began to guess what it might mean to live from the heart instead of the head, and I began to feel movements of the heart which told me more surely what I wanted than any making of lists.

A Life of One's Own, Joanna Field

1 If I had no one close at hand to help or encourage me, I also had no one to blame. I was responsible for who I was and how I felt.

Always a Woman, Kaylan Pickford

I used to stay awake nights, then get up and journal or write letters in a futile attempt to resolve something beyond my control; the convolutions and wasted energy of pretzel logic.

Sally H.

Anything I've ever let go of has claw marks on it.
Sally E.

It is not necessary to deny another's reality in order to affirm my own.
Women's Reality, Anne Wilson Schaef

T he truth was that I had internalized society's unserious estimate of all that was female — including myself. This was low self-esteem, not logic.

Revolution From Within, Gloria Steinem

Suffering is not reduced by refusing to face it or by wallowing in it but only by accepting it, surrendering to it, and letting the natural healing processes take root and unfold.

Loneliness and Love, Clark E. Moustakas

Self-development is a higher duty than self-sacrifice. The thing which most retards and militates against women's self-development is self-sacrifice.

In a Different Voice, Carol Gilligan

W

E WOMEN ARE PROFICIENT AT GIVING,
BUT RECEIVING OFTEN SEEMS STRANGE AND,
SOMEHOW, NOT RIGHT.

WOMEN'S BOOK OF COURAGE

Self-healing begins with making our own decisions — about what we wear, what we do, who we are — and deciding that we will be true to ourselves.

Each Day a New Beginning

In the legend there is relief from the enemy, sorrow is turned into gladness, mourning into holiday. In life, only some of this is possible.

Weave of Women, E.M. Broner

Faith—is the Pierless Bridge
Supporting what We see
Unto the Scene that We do not—
                    Emily Dickinson

Only in growth, reform, and change, paradoxically enough, is true security to be found.
Anne Morrow Lindbergh

FEAR BECOMES AN ALLY WHICH
WHISPERS THAT WE ARE COMING
TO OUR EDGE, TO UNPLUMBED DEPTHS,
TO THE SPACE IN WHICH ALL GROWTH OCCURS.

Healing Into Life and Death, STEPHEN LEVINE

Why do I tarry in this narrow confined frame, when life, all life with all its joys, is open to me?

Leo Tolstoy

The "still, small voice" is heard more in the silence beyond, around, and beneath language than it is in the cacophony of incessant sound.

Women's Book of Courage

 It is an act of courage to acknowledge our own uncertainty and sit with it for awhile.
The Dance of Intimacy, Harriet Goldhor Lerner

Many of us are frightened by the unknown. Yet deep within us all are reserves of strength and courage that can lead us on.

Ended Beginnings, Claudia Panuthos/Catherine Romeo

The greatest fault that can happen to human relationships: they become impatient.

Rilke on Love and Other Difficulties, Rainer Maria Rilke

If we have no peace, it is because
we have forgotten that we belong to each other.
MOTHER TERESA

The hardest part of living alone is exactly like the hardest part of the relationship — weathering its moments of distance, its failures of insight and strength, accepting that at certain times one is powerless to affect the sadness of another — that one is sometimes powerless in the face of one's own sadness.

Kiss Sleeping Beauty Goodbye, Modonna Kolbenschlag

WHERE LANGUAGE AND NAMING ARE POWER, silence is oppression, is violence.

Diving into the Wreck, Adrienne Rich

If I had influence with the good fairy who is supposed to preside over christening of all children, I should ask that her gift to each child in the world be a sense of wonder so indestructible that it would last throughout life.

Chop Wood, RACHEL CARSON

S o much of our life is a reflection of what has just occurred rather than a direct participation in the unfolding moment.
Healing into Life and Death, Stephen Levine

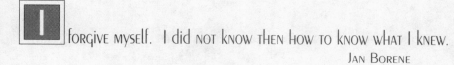 forgive myself. I did not know then how to know what I knew.

JAN BORENE

always wanted to be somebody, but I should have been more specific.
Lily Tomlin and Jane Wagner

Not to the future, but to the Fuchsia.
GERTRUDE STEIN

It is the image in the mind that binds us to our lost treasures, but it is the loss that shapes the image.

Colette

How simple life is. Live with awareness, not by rules or conditioning or thinking or shoulds or shouldn'ts.
Don't push the River, Barry Stevens

If you measure success in terms of
praise and criticism, your anxiety will be endless.
J. Heider

Risk, Risk, anything! Care no more for the opinions of others, for those voices. Do the hardest thing on earth for you. Act for yourself. Face the truth.

Katherine Mansfield

When you open up your life to the living,
all things come spilling in on you.
And you're floating like a river,
the Changer and the Changed.
You've got to spill some over.
Waterfall, Cris Williamson

Friendship is the inexpressible comfort of feeling safe with a person having neither to weigh thoughts nor measure words.

George Eliot

A faithful friend is a sturdy shelter.
(She) that has found one has found a treasure.
Ecclesiasticus 6:14, A Hebrew proverb

B ut friendship provides the setting for forms of pleasure and personal growth that may not be found on the wilder shores of love.
Necessary Losses, Judith Viorst

I said to the almond tree, "Speak to me of God."
The almond tree blossomed.

Nikos Kazantzakis

The sisters of mercy, they are not departed or gone.
They were waiting for me when I thought that I just can't go on.
Judy Collins

I will fold you in my arms,
like the white-winged dove,
Shine in your soul; Your spirit is crying.

Cris Williamson

Genuine love not only respects the individuality of the other but actually seeks to cultivate it, even at the risk of separation or loss.
The Road Less Traveled, M. Scott Peck

As selfishness and complaint pervert
and cloud the mind, so love with its joy
clears and sharpens the vision.

Helen Keller

The worst part of success is
trying to find someone who is happy for you.
Bette Midler

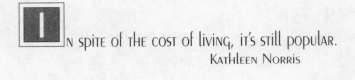In spite of the cost of living, it's still popular.
KATHLEEN NORRIS

WHEN WE STEP AWAY FROM OUR EGO AND develop a selfless posture toward life, we'll find serenity in the midst of any turmoil.
EACH DAY A NEW BEGINNING

Finally, the lessons of impermanence taught me this: loss constitutes an odd kind of fullness; despair empties out into an unquenchable appetite for life.

The Solace of Open Spaces, Gretel Ehrlich

If you survive long enough, you're revered — rather like an old building.
KATHARINE HEPBURN

To try to control your life is the coward's way out.
It means there are no adventures, surprises, or magical turning points.
The Courage of Conviction, Rita Mae Brown

Part of sobriety is learning to live with
ambiguity, paradox, and unanswered questions.
Women, Sex, and Addiction, Charlotte Davis Kasl

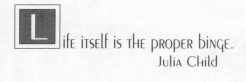 Life itself is the proper binge.
Julia Child

The people in one's life are like the pillars on one's porch you see life through. And sometimes they hold you up, and sometimes they lean on you, and sometimes it is just enough to know they're standing by.

Some Men are More Perfect Than Others, Merle Shain

A dopt the pace of nature; her secret is patience.
Ralph Waldo Emerson

One must believe in the possibility of happiness in order to be happy, and now I believe in it. While one has life one must live and be happy.

War and Peace, Leo Tolstoy

The real voyage of discovery consists not in seeking new landscapes, but in having new eyes.

Marcel Proust

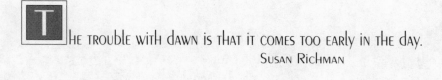

The trouble with dawn is that it comes too early in the day.

Susan Richman

It is good to have an end to journey towards;
but it is the journey that matters in the end.

Ursula K. LeGuin